I0620467

Crystal Harmony of Healing

Verses of Inner Peace, Transformation, and Sacred Connection

ESOTERIC POETRY
BY
Michaela

Dedication

For those who wander the winding paths of nature, may each step inspire a deeper connection with the world around us. In moments of perplexity, may the beauty of creation remind us of our resilience and the joy that lies within the journey. This compilation is a tribute to the spirit of exploration and the transformative power of the natural world. Additionally, I would like to acknowledge Susan for her amazing artwork.

Contents

About the Author

Michaela is a versatile artist, seamlessly blending her talents as a writer, singer-songwriter, and brand developer. Her music, a fusion of inspirational lyrics and light rock melodies, is featured on three CDs. As an author, she has published poetry compilations exploring New Age topics. Her esoteric approach, drawing on ancient wisdom and the beauty of nature, shines through in all her creative endeavors. In addition to her artistic pursuits, she is the founder of the CrystalOil essential oils brand.

HEALING TREE

Beneath the celestial gaze of God's creative hand, the Healing Tree arises; birthed in the ethereal realm, perfected in symphony and flawless fruition. It stands as a beacon of light amidst the somber embrace of darkness and land, a fleeting moment of divine grace for humanity to seize.

1

MICHAELA

Within the sacred garden, every tree and creation blooms in abundant splendor, a testament to God's boundless beauty. Influenced by the guiding hand of Jupiter, the arboreal majesty breathes life, reigning over realms of love and prophecy. The eagle, messenger of Jupiter, embodies swiftness and sovereignty akin to the sun's radiant rule.

Amidst this verdant tapestry, the oak stands tall, a symbol of unwavering stability, while the mandrake, with its mystical essence, bestows healing and purity upon all who seek its solace. Grapes, blessed by the lunar influence, embody the strength of the mind, fertility, and the ecstasy of abundance and prosperity.

In the graceful dance of the deer, we glimpse the soul's aspiration, swift and elegant, embodying the essence of life's eternal journey towards the divine.

In the gentle flight of the dove, we find the embodiment of peace and wisdom, a herald of purity and the promise of new beginnings. With grace and swiftness, the deer symbolizes the soul's aspirations towards a life of beauty and purpose. Amidst the shadows, the crow stands as a symbol of foretold destinies, a harbinger of the darkness that precedes creation, yet also a guide to the known realities and the changes that await. And in the majestic presence of the phoenix, we witness celestial rule and the wondrous power of regeneration from within.

DEPTH

In the depths of the earth, a seed of pure gold lies dormant, a reflection of the eternal realm's essence, quietly forming below the surface. Bathed in the warm embrace of the sun's rays, it awaits its moment of potential realization, nurtured by the diligence of a superior soul. Like a grain of sand nestled within the earth's embrace, like a child in his mothers embrace, the treasure of greatness patiently awaits, slowly taking shape and evolving towards its destined form.

ADORNED

The gates open, and she emerges, adorned by the gentle caress of moonlight. His presence, a beacon of renewed hope, glistens in the night. Recalling his own endeavors, he finds solace in silence, knowing he reigns in her realm. This night, tinged with subtle nuances illuminated by the moon, their lives intertwine in a tapestry of enchantment. All that has transpired is theirs alone to understand, while the future remains cloaked in mystery. From afar she appears, attired gloriously, her army surrounds her. Vision ahead, frees from bondage, freedom elating her heart. Her army protects, alive she feels, The binds of the past dissipating.

REASON

As Reason sits enthroned, she is also guiding our actions; a symphony of motion echoes through humanity. Mighty are her endeavors, shaping the hearts and minds of all who share this journey. Within, battles for survival unfold, each struggle a testament to their evolution. Like angels in constant vigilance, they strive for permanence amidst the ever-changing tides of existence. Above and below, hopes and dreams take root, slowly molding a new reality with each subtle shift. As reason stands firm; in motion are her responses, shaping the will of mankind. Mighty are endeavors, continually influencing the hearts and minds of the collective. Rare and majestic are the battles within, where survival is at stake, molding us into who we are becoming. Like guardians in the heavens, that witness changes unfold, fighting for the permanence of wills. Above and below, hopes and aspirations take root, like the gradual transformation of motion forming a new reality.

TRANSCENDANCE

Divided yet whole; love illuminates the path, reviving hopes within my soul. Ordeals of survival serve as reminders of unmet needs, yet amidst division, my destiny remains intertwined. Claiming breath over the tests of time is a life's arduous journey, drawing strength from an eternal source. The earth awaits completion, embracing all, and in unity, two souls find supremacy, amplifying and receiving from one another.

A FACE

Countenance is as a union of idealized perfection, merging under the moon's gentle glow. To love is to transcend, though losses linger. I find solace in surrendering to your will, seeking continuity within the boundless generosity of the sky. I yearn for my true grasp, embracing the ideals of truths I admire, though you seem beyond this moment, our becoming is infinite.

INSPIRATION

Inspiration flows abundantly as truth, breathing life into the desolate ruins of existence. The mighty winds of destiny reign over the heavens, inscribing the fate of man upon the earth. Like a pale heroine enduring with reason, she confronts the desperation of her existence, steadfast in the pursuit of transcendence.

CREATION

Spirit, mind, and soul descend into the four worlds: creation, emanation, formation, and illumination. Earth, water, air, and fire; the elements from which all is shaped; from the rivers, waters flow into the garden. The blazing sun, casting its influence, while the horizon remains tranquil, echoes with silent forms of ancient truths. The germ, the seed, the inception of spiritual potential; undisturbed wholeness intertwines as one. Life is infused from a primal source, a celestial essence, from which all emerges pure and whole.

THE EARTH

The element is earth, a dragon to be vanquished; the path fraught with peril for those who stray. For the plight of man is daunting; man prepares himself as he sets forth on his journey, sword at his side. A pentacle, a symbol of triumph, a convergence of the elements, a beacon of hope. Carrying his own burdens, he masters his direction and intent, summoning his inner strength. The earth, round and complete, epitomizes the completeness of creation, as he walks on.

AN ANGEL

An angel, brought forth to fruition from realms on high, through wishes and desires. The thoughts of humanity, creations and realms, exist within the celestial sphere of true aspirations. Existing eternally, never waning, the angels watch over days and nights without end, steadfast in their guardianship. For the Like of a sleeping child, innocent and pure.

MANKIND

And mankind resumes Tasks and simple endeavors, sustaining the willful existence of humanity. The undercurrents of a complex reality are met with simple responses, willingly bestowed. Yet mysteries persist; each step unveiled in due time, leaving its toll. Man's vulnerability veiled by his earthly efforts; his courageous responses commendable. Progression of wills and actions leading to her love. And Resting by the roadside, weariness from battles endured, he awaits his fate. Amidst losses suffered and victories celebrated, he learns anew from a wellspring of wisdom. And the changes that ripple beneath the surface take shape as novelty, the world responding in turn. Consequences, transformed by diligence, offer solace, for changes take root and bring forth their effects.

A DREAMER

Love persists, and within its embrace, a dream unfurls, each moment a universe unto itself, revealing an untold reality. A vision held by greatness, laying the groundwork for possibility, enduring even as we stumble. Breaking free from the shackles of misguided notions, we strive for improvement, guided by the true essence of what is right. As we break the chains of deception, the true essence of worth illuminates our path.

Above, the noble crown of existence awaits, rewarding the steps of the genuine seeker. Adoration becomes an eternal wellspring of devotion and craftsmanship. Symbols emerge as pillars of timeless foundation, stirring and enlightening the living, offering glimpses of hope.

WITHIN

Within us lies the power to heal, for faith's might is boundless, guiding us towards faithful responses and timely resolutions that pave our way. Amidst the fading of life, we capture meaning; faces transform, even in moments of dismay. The quality of our existence hinges upon unity, as we gather together to bring forth order. Tranquility envelops those who seek and yearn, and healing is as clear forms of creation , choices await in the unity of hope and real steps.

A mission unfolds, touched by the gentle stirring of another soul. Each attempt to restore order is a testament to the progress of life, for possibility forever lingers. Motion reminds us of change and novelty, as we navigate trials to uncover deeper truths. Water, an endless font of giving; the sun, ceaselessly warming; air, in perpetual motion; earth, eternally containing.

MANSIONS OF THE MOON

The pale white horse of revelation rides through the night, traversing the dunes of time as the starry sky stretches towards the horizon. The moon, in its myriad forms, unveils each mansion and chamber, guiding us through the phases of our journey. Angels stand watch over each stage, aiding in our recreation amidst troubled times. In the harvest of success lies unbound treasure, and like a ray of light, the pale white horse of revelation gallops through the night.

THE EQUINOX

On the horizon, at a solitary point, we await the equinox, a vision of nature awaited with bated breath. Desire and anticipation for a longed-for outcome stretch this moment into never-ending trials. In faint recollection, I cling to memories, to prevailing hope. My dreams of eternity, remind of you and your hopes . We converge at a singular point of merit, loss, and need intertwined.

AN EXPRESSION OF WILL

A will that radiates, A breath of sorrow stirs ; I plead; I imagine. I remember , I express, conveying elements of truth. A creative force bestows ; As the rain falls I remains inspired, unhindered. As immaculate as heaven's design, untouched by influence. Each attempt holds the pain of remembering, awaiting an outcome. Expression, the amalgamation of all, awaits. Each expression descends to its own realm of existence. Each power, most encompassing, creates and fulfills its destiny. As a master plan unfolds, the universe of possibility awaits, with keys to gates. Descending from on high come the blessings, manifesting as illuminating rays. I sense the changes, understanding, allowing for possibility, for the granting of will, creating fertile ground. Neither too far nor too near; I grasp and hold onto a life that brings solace. A middle ground, firm and just, upheld with unwavering faith. Creating and shaping, leading to where will exists, and intentions persist. The eternal, grounded and realized, with many findings shelter where clarity reigns. Yellow, like the sun, symbolizes hope, and the angels, uncountable, praise creation as they set the throne. In the midst, a center held steadfast, birthing new realities as wonders unfold.

IN THE HEAVENS

All forms, thoughts, and creations, none arose, before the foundations. Pillars of brass, origins of conception, the porch of a temple, existing within. On the entrance pillars, water, contained. The gifts of nature, the gifts of man, existing, in total harmony. A life conceived, a lifeline represented; the life of a man, and all its consequences. The letters from sapphire blazed supremely.

FROM VENUS TO MARS

Extending my abilities, my feelings and aspirations, expression I attempt to convey, as I venture beyond my known foundations. Separated, yet still reaching, for the objects of my desires, I stand guard over boundaries, as my will persists. From Venus to Mars, I endure.

ONE

A lion reigns, one with nature, commanding over a world endured by all. Forces surge, overcoming doubt in this moment, and healing prevails. Chains that bind will shatter, for a light still shines, beckoning us forward. Destiny, written and unwavering, Prevails, urging.

THE EARTH The element of earth, a dragon to be slayed, A treacherous path for those who stray. Yet man, in preparation, embarks on his journey, With sword in hand. A pentacle, a sign of victory, Unifying the elements, brings hope. Bearing his burdens, mastering direction and intent, Man summons his strength. The earth, round and complete, Symbolizes the completeness of creation.

METALS

Metals reflecting man's nature, body and spirit united, forming a unified whole. Each metal upholds and adorns the fate of man. Gold, representing the material reality of the glorious Sun, Silver, the sensation of the world, sanctioned by the Moon, Lead, judgment and discernment under the light of Saturn, Tin, wisdom relieving hardship under the influence of Jupiter, Iron, reactions to the battles of Mars, Copper, demanding character under the beauty of Venus, Mercury, healing under the light of Mercury.

URGING

A crown above creation, a foundation below, Shattered by tensions of man. Male and female, placed on earth, devastated, their expressions proving the intent of survival.

Ancient father, ancient mother, still hoping and urging, For the needs of creation. Darkness and light, absolute yet separate, Emanating and existing, awaiting each other.

Giving away is letting go, and starting over is also. Between darkness and light, Existence continues, each existing on its own.

THE WHEELS OF THE CHARIOT

The wheels of the chariot essential, blaze and gleam, holding a sustaining sphere. Each wheel holds a world, initiating and bringing forth possibilities. Alone incomplete, yet together creating, vision of flawless and perfected plane of existence, together complete in Royalty.

REFLECTION

The soul creates, vibrations resonate, reflecting an existence, a reality lived. Resonating vibrations leave lasting impressions, Creations and formations reflect ideals. Results are everlasting, remembered by the world.

MOTION

As the earth turns, holding its creative fire, firmly grounded, motion remains clear and true. Abundant and firmly planted, a world containing, Recombining elements in different measures. For all things formed and actions planned, Creation offers endless possibilities. Astral fire, heavenly waters, comforting air, protecting earth, Recombining elements shaping new realities.As waves return, urging on, Improvement reciprocated like a ray of light. Strength of man awaits Journey of Healing and Embracing the Abundance. Each aspect internalized.

EVERY RIDER

Every rider is alone, pledging for solitude, As the heavens await his sorrows. Protected in solitude, anticipating, His return awaited, remembered by all. Amidst turmoil, understanding, Leading his horse forward. One is eternal, two represents male and female, Three forever holding, directing life outward. Eternal motion, cubes and lines, circles, Completing and describing, holding the unity of two. One is the first cause, the seed giving continuity.

MICHAELA

I BREATHE

I breathe for a moment, a breath of fresh air, Clarity of soul known for an instant. Luck felt as a gift from higher creation, Sustained momentarily, a breath of tranquility. A glimpse of gracefulness, guiding through another day. My will proves my existence, A Journey of Healing and Embracing the Abundance Within My desire proves my intent, A Journey of Healing and Embracing the Abundance Within beliefs prove my actions. My womb protects, nurtures, upholds, A state of mind, soundness of heart, stability of spirit, Soulful existence.

A TAPESTRY

A tapestry to remind, to inquire of forgotten truths, Colors and forms of many lives. The dove adorned for peace, The eagle depicting strength and honor, The lion reminding of fruitfulness. Aspirations for transcendental truth, Hopes curing the soul. Resolutions remembered, lives of the eager held, Success of discernment, healing of the people, in the midst. Union of male and female forces, potentiating desires, Continuity, and a day lived as waves break and land yields. Ships remain, built with eternity's promise. In the silence, we find clarity, our connection to the earth a source of strength, guiding us on our quest. Memories of the journey etch themselves in the light, urging us to forge ahead, seeking the essence of our being. As we navigate the trails illuminated before us, our desires merge with destiny, crafting a narrative of perseverance and discovery, each step a testament to the unwavering spirit that guides us. In the tapestry of time, your image is a beacon, a constellation of memories that guide my way. Chosen moments, illuminated by the essence of our connection, weave a narrative of unity and divergence. The perfection of our encounters, captured in the fleeting dance of light and shadow, serves as a reminder of what was and what may yet be, as we traverse the continuum of existence, seeking the harmony that binds us.

THE HEAVEN OF MERCURY

Filled to the boundaries, populated shores, Success mysteries unraveled in Mercury's heaven. Eloquence underlying, esoteric sciences, A moral force, successful tones of prevalence.

THE HEAVEN OF THE MOON

Changes and doubts, failures and questions, Reflections of man's existence. Luminosity of contemplation, imagination, and creation, Reflecting on the endless tries of daily hope.

Witnessing anticipation, reflecting on endless tries, The moon, witness to never-ending plights, surrendering seas. Eternal motion, cubes and lines, circles, Completing and describing, holding the unity of two.

COLORS

PARTIALITY-14

Green for health, luck, and fortune, Fertility in Venus existing, Yellow for attraction and charm, Captivation in Leo by the sun's rays.

Orange for adaptability and expression, Courage in Virgo under Mercury.

Red for passion and strength, Protection in Aries under Mars.

Black, the color of banishment, yet of all, Protection in Scorpio under Saturn and earth.

SPRING

Spring brings wonder, uplifting the spirit, Melting ice and flowing streams, Bringing warmth and sentiments of return. Fury steel stubbornly keeping, commanding return of primary intent. For nature, willed long ago, charted ways fixed like the stars.

Eternity infused in a true creation, blessed and hallowed, Brought down from an eternal source, sanctified in vision. Before union, before conception, the higher boat of creative fire, Encompassing an all-encompassing God.

After Night Falls

Beneath a tapestry of starlight, hues of deepest blue shimmer like precious gems. Night descends, its embrace deepening the sky, a dance of shadow and luminescence. Dawn's approach whispers of renewal, a cycle of darkness into light, each moment a step towards the new day's promise. Memories of falls past linger, yet within the cloak of night, hope and remembrance persist. We ponder stillness, the possibility of redemption from our stumbles, a silent vigil until the morrow's light.

As Day Breaks

With the break of day, it is your essence I perceive, enveloping me, dismantling and reassembling every part of my being with an urgent call. In fleeting moments, I summon your presence, piecing us back together in a dance of creation and reformation. The dawn reveals my transformation, and in its light, I still find you, the cornerstone of my existence. You are the anchor in my tempest, the beacon as I soar, the marvel in my existence, unyielding, ever beginning anew at the precipice of time.

Light of Ascent

As we embark on this new era, we seek enlightenment, actively shaping our destinies. The dawn of spiritual ascension beckons, inviting us to harmonize with our inner gifts. In understanding our desires and dreams, we journey towards our ideal selves, navigating the currents of life with wisdom and purpose. Each step, guided by the subtle energies of the universe, illuminates our path, teaching us the synchrony of body, mind, and spirit. Our journey is a testament to the power of focused intent, a celebration of the harmony within.

Perfect Whole

In the meditation of being, where body and mind unite, we rediscover ancient wisdom, as timeless as the oak. Each thought, each breath, a stroke on the canvas of existence, blending into a masterpiece of wholeness. Our journey through time, a sequence of deliberate steps, liberates us from our bonds, propelling us towards the ethereal. Above us, the sky forms a canvas, where clouds swirl into a symphony of silver and blue, a reflection of our innermost aspirations, merging into the perfection of the cosmos.

In Place

Aligned with the cosmos, we stand ready, the fabric of the universe intricately woven with our destinies. As the mountains release their sorrows to nourish the earth below, we too shed our past, embracing the potential of now. Nature's majesty, a mirror of our inner landscapes, guides our steps, aligning our energy with the universal flow. Past and present converge, shaping our unique gifts, as we stand poised on the threshold of the unknown, our futures brightly envisaged in the constellations above.

A Break

In the heart of the storm, a clearing emerges, a reconciliation with the night. New horizons beckon, pain and fear dissolve under the day's forgiving light. Through verdant meadows and radiant passages, I hasten towards a dawn of my own making, where echoes of your presence guide me through life's labyrinth. A pause, a breath, and the world unfold anew, a mosaic of possibilities where existence and longing intertwine, crafting the tapestry of our collective destiny.

Here and Now

In the vast expanse of time and space, we journey, bearing the weight of moments lost, yet in the here and now, love becomes our guiding star. Amidst heartaches traversed and truths unveiled, we stand resilient, a beacon amidst life's tempests. Safe within the present, propelled by life's undying force, we navigate through storms, our bonds unbroken by time's relentless surge. The present moment heals, transforming each step into a testament of our resilience, forging a path anew from the wilderness of our trials. As your name whispers across my thoughts, a bridge forms between us, questioning our existence in the vast tapestry of now. Facing our fears, embracing the possibility of separation, I wonder of eternity.

Incarnation

As we usher in a new epoch, the cosmos beckons, receptive to our vibrations, urging us to forge ahead, to become one with the universe. Shedding fears and doubts, we traverse the deserts of anticipation, reaching towards the dreams that flicker on the horizon, bridging the chasm between aspiration and realization. Our destiny is not written in the stars but forged through our earthly pursuits, as we strive to mend the tapestry of our past, guided by the unique frequencies of our being, destined to illuminate the world.

In Sight

Perched on the brink, he stands, enveloped by the protective embrace of the clouds, his fate a beacon in the mist. The azure clarity of the topaz sky and the verdant depths below mark the canvas of his transformation. Each step, a testament of evolution, memories of dreams past fuel his resolve. As the heavens roar, the path ahead unfolds, each stride aligned with destiny, his essence merging with the infinite, rejuvenated with every breath.

As the Road Turns

From chaos to serenity, the journey unfolds, revealing the depths of the astral realms and the truths they hold. Foundations are shaken, yet resilience emerges, guiding us through the labyrinth of existence. Shielded by ideals, we navigate the continuum of time and space, each quantum leaps as day conquered pain healed for a moment, as a new dawn envisioned. As rain cleanses sorrow, our path diverges, leading us towards uncharted horizons, where expectations dance on the wings of hope. In the realm of shadows and light, we find our reflection, a confluence of contradictions, seeking solace in the in-between. Each step, a dance with destiny, a negotiation with the self, as we navigate the twilight of our being. The warrior within perceives a life of balance, embracing the turbulence and tranquility that define our existence. In this liminal space, a new reality is born, ascending above the dualities that bind us, guided by the crimson sun at its zenith.

Swiftness in Time

In the realm of the now, actions ripple with purpose, sculpting the fabric of existence from the intangible. Aspirations take flight, fueled by the synergy of collective endeavors, each moment a mosaic of potential. From the void emerges a path, illuminated by the spectrum of possibilities, as relationships weave the tapestry of our shared journey, dreams manifesting into tangible reality, anchored in the unity of our intentions.

Grateful

Beneath the canopy of the night, the strength of years manifests, wisdom gleaned from the ether, binding souls across the expanse of time. The ancient tongue, a bridge between worlds, propels us forward, as we conquer new realms, borne on the wings of light. In gratitude, we traverse the infinite, guided by the stars, our destiny a symphony of light and shadow, forever intertwined with the fabric of the universe.

Interpretation

Across the vast expanse of the cosmos, we seek clarity, navigating the multitude of paths that destiny unfolds. Each interpretation, a mirror of the soul, as the tides of time sculpt the shores of our existence. In the dance of creation and destruction, we find renewal, a sprouting of hope in the desolate landscape of our trials. Our journey, a testament to the resilience of the human spirit, is guided by the immutable laws of the universe, forever seeking the light.

WONDERINGS OF HOPE

In the confluence of fate and will, mysteries unravel, revealing the intricate dance of existence. Boundaries dissolve as we leap beyond the known, guided by a force greater than ourselves. In the rainfall, in the ascent of flight, we find freedom, a connection to the ancient rhythms that govern our journey. As the world unfolds in a kaleidoscope of possibility, we stand at the crossroads of destiny, clothed in the enigma of our own making, ever seeking the truth that lies just beyond reach. Within the crucible of the soul, consciousness expands, a flash of insight illuminating the darkness. As we navigate the abyss, transformation beckons, drawing forth forms and ideas that transcend the mundane. In this alchemy of spirit, we find our essence, a beacon of hope in the tumult of existence, guiding us towards the dawn of a new understanding, where the mysteries of the universe unfold in the light of our awakening.

Dark Night of the Soul

In the depths of despair, a light persists, guiding us through the veil of night. As the fabric of our being is tested, a bond emerges, stronger for its trials, a beacon in the darkness. Together, we endure the long night, finding solace in the promise of a new day. As dawn breaks, the land is transformed, hope reborn in the symphony of life, an ode to the resilience of the soul, forever seeking the light.

In the vast expanse of time and space, we journey, bearing the weight of moments lost, yet in the here and now, love becomes our guiding star. Amidst heartaches traversed and truths unveiled, we stand resilient, a beacon amidst life's tempests. Safe within the present, propelled by life's undying force, we navigate through storms, our bonds unbroken by time's relentless surge. The present moment heals, transforming each step into a testament of our resilience, forging a path anew from the wilderness of our trials. As your name whispers across my thoughts, a bridge forms between us, questioning our existence in the vast tapestry of now. Facing our fears, embracing the possibility of renewal, I wonder, will you stand by me?

In Sight

Perched on the brink, he stands, enveloped by the protective embrace of the clouds, his fate a beacon in the mist. The azure clarity of the topaz sky and the verdant depths below mark the canvas of his transformation. Each step, a testament to his evolution, memories of dreams past fuel his resolve. As the heavens roar, the path ahead unfolds, each stride aligned with destiny, his essence merging with the infinite, rejuvenated with every breath.

As the Road Turns

From chaos to serenity, the journey unfolds, revealing the depths of the astral realms and the truths they hold. Foundations are shaken, yet resilience emerges, guiding us through the labyrinth of existence. Shielded by ideals, we navigate the continuum of time and space, each quantum leap a lesson learned, a hurt healed, a new dawn envisioned. As rain cleanses sorrow, our path diverges, leading us towards uncharted horizons, where expectations dance on the wings of hope.

In Between

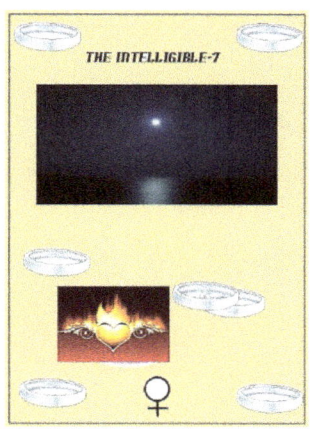

In the realm of shadows and light, we find our reflection, a confluence of contradictions, seeking solace in the in-between. Each step, a dance with destiny, a negotiation with the self, as we navigate the twilight of our being. The warrior within perceives a life of balance, embracing the turbulence and tranquility that define our existence. In this liminal space, a new reality is born, ascending above the dualities that bind us, guided by the crimson sun at its zenith.In the realm of the now, actions ripple with purpose, sculpting the fabric of existence from the intangible. Aspirations take flight, fueled by the synergy of collective endeavors, each moment a mosaic of potential. From the void emerges a path, illuminated by the spectrum of possibilities, as relationships weave the tapestry of our shared journey, dreams manifesting into tangible reality, anchored in the unity of our intentions.

Focus

In the silence, we find clarity, our connection to the earth a source of strength, guiding us on our quest. Memories of the journey etch themselves in the light, urging us to forge ahead, seeking the essence of our being. As we navigate the trails illuminated before us, our desires merge with destiny, crafting a narrative of perseverance and discovery, each step a testament to the unwavering spirit that guides us.

Remembering

In the tapestry of time, your image is a beacon, a constellation of memories that guide my way. Chosen moments, illuminated by the essence of our connection, weave a narrative of unity and divergence. The perfection of our encounters, captured in the fleeting dance of light and shadow, serves as a reminder of what was and what may yet be, as we traverse the continuum of existence, seeking the harmony that binds us.

Interpretation

Across the vast expanse of the cosmos, we seek clarity, navigating the multitude of paths that destiny unfolds. Each interpretation, a mirror of the soul, as the tides of time sculpt the shores of our existence. In the dance of creation and destruction, we find renewal, a sprouting of hope in the desolate landscape of our trials. Our journey, a testament to the resilience of the human spirit, is guided by the immutable laws of the universe, forever seeking the light.

A MYSTERY

In the confluence of fate and will, mysteries unravel, revealing the intricate dance of existence. Boundaries dissolve as we leap beyond the known, guided by a force greater than ourselves. In the rainfall, in the ascent of flight, we find freedom, a connection to the ancient rhythms that govern our journey. As the world unfolds in a kaleidoscope of possibility, we stand at the crossroads of destiny, clothed in the enigma of our own making, ever seeking the truth that lies just beyond reach. Within the crucible of the soul, consciousness expands, a flash of insight illuminating the darkness. As we navigate the abyss, transformation beckons, drawing forth forms and ideas that transcend the mundane. In this alchemy of spirit, we find our essence, a beacon of hope in the tumult of existence, guiding us towards the dawn of a new understanding, where the mysteries of the universe unfold in the light of our awakening, and why is all a mystery.

A Tempest

You arrived, then departed, A day's journey across my heart, Like a tempest raging upon the ocean, Leaving echoes in its wake. Wandering through the continuum of time and space, Epiphanies emerge from the depths of moments once passed, Within the present's embrace, love anchors steadfast. Heartaches, those wayward guides, lead us through life's maze, Truth, in its essence, shines amidst the tempest's craze. In the sanctuary of now, sheltered from life's relentless gales, We find solace, as destiny's ship through tempest sails, Bound by the eternal shores where past and future intertwine, In the realm of the immediate, where every moment is a sign. Bold steps forward, each a testament to our spirit's quest, Crafting anew, from the ruins, a life that's truly blessed. Emerging from the shadows, a single truth we ascertain, In the dance of existence, every step counts in the endless refrain. And so I rise, Fear of the end, a shadow fading in the light of our resolve, Healing, a possible grace, in love's mystery we dissolve. A storm above me descending .

Incarnations

As we step into the dawn of a new era, with the cosmos echoing our vibrations, Our journey unfolds, a testament to our soul's aspirations. Breaking free from the chains of fear and doubt, We navigate the deserts of our quests, towards realms where our dreams may be met. In the vista of our ambitions, where form and essence converge, We take bold strides towards destiny, as our spirits surge. Birthed anew in the crucible of life, each challenge a chance to mend, Our essence spirals towards that primal beginning, where all stories blend once again.

Within Reach

Beyond the abyss, he stands, between earth and sky, With clouds above as guardians, and a destiny that never lies. The sea below, a mirror of his soul's deepest hue, In every step, a transformation, as his vision comes into view. A dream once whispered in the echoes of his heart, Now unfolds before him, a new chapter ready to start. As the storm brews above, a symbol of many choices he'll navigate, Each step forward, a testament of change . From chaos to clarity, the journey unfolds, Quantum leaps through realms, as the story of growth is told. Broken codes and realms unveiled, a path through the astral plane, Each step a discovery, as wisdom from the stars we gain. Pain and sorrow, now mere echoes of a rain-soaked past, As the road twists and turns, towards a future vast he steps towards.

Between

In the dance of shadow and light, where life's mysteries are spun, We find our tales intertwined, under the same sun. In this space of flux, where truths and dreams collide, A new reality is crafted, where hope and courage reside. As we traverse this spectrum, where every shade is a choice, Our voices merge into a chorus, each note a reason to rejoice.

Swiftness in Time

In the realm of moments, where actions and destiny align, Our lives unfold in symphony, each note a design divine. As we dance through the cycles, where past and future blend, In the light of understanding, our spirits ascend. A journey through dimensions, where every step is a key, Unlocking the mysteries of existence, setting our souls free.

TIME AND SPACE

In the quest for understanding, where heart and earth entwine, We seek the essence of being, in every sign and line. As trails blaze before us, in the light of quests divine, We hold onto our dreams, in the dance of time. In the tapestry of existence, where memories and dreams intertwine, Each moment a reflection, of a journey that's both yours and mine. As we navigate the currents, where past and future meet, In the heart of now, our stories complete. As the storm recedes, leaving clarity in its wake, We find strength in the journey, with every step we take. Bound by the threads of time, where destiny and courage meld, In the dance of the cosmos, our stories are spelled. Through the lens of time, where every path leads to a new dawn, We discover the essence of being, in the world we've drawn. As the shores of understanding beckon, with each wave that breaks, In the realm of possibilities, our spirit awakes. In the maze of existence, where every path is a clue, We seek the heart of mystery, in everything we pursue. As the world unfolds before us, in a spectrum of light and shade, In the quest for understanding, our journey is made. Beyond the bounds of time, where thoughts and dreams take flight, We soar towards understanding, in the realm of endless light. As the cosmos whispers secrets, in the fabric of the night, In the quest for enlightenment, our spirits ignite.

Dark Night to Light

Through the depths of darkness, where hope and despair entwine, We find strength in the journey, with every step divine. As dawn breaks the horizon, a new chapter begins to unfold, In the light of understanding, our stories are told.No more glances backward, where the shadows of the past reside, Ahead lies the essence of being, in the light we confide. In the dance of the present, where every moment is a key, We find our path forward, where our spirits are free. Past the edge of the known, where dreams and reality blend, A city of old tales, of beginnings and ends. As the arc of history bends towards the light of understanding, We find our place in the story, our destinies expanding. Light illuminating

In the realm of new beginnings, where the fabric of time is woven anew, We find our reflections in the mirror of the cosmos, a perspective true. As the essence of being merges with the flow of time, In the dance of the universe, our spirits align. And darkness dissipates.

Realms of IDEALS

In the realm of ideals, where the stars whisper tales of yore, We find our purpose in the cosmos, our spirits soar. As we reach towards the heavens, where dreams are born, In the fabric of the cosmos, our destinies are sworn. In the space between worlds, where the heart and heavens meet, We find our balance in the cosmos, our journey complete. As we navigate the spectrum of existence, where every shade is a key, In the dance of the cosmos, our spirits are free.

Changes

As the world turns beneath us, where past and present intertwine, We find our path through the cosmos, our destinies aligned. As the fabric of time weaves tales of renewal and decay, In the heart of the cosmos, our spirits find their way. In the dance of the cosmos, where every step is a note in the symphony of life, We find our harmony in the balance of light and strife. As we traverse the spectrum of existence, where every shade is a revelation, In the fabric of the cosmos, we find our hope after sorrow. In the dance of eternity, where the cycles of time intertwine, We find our place in the cosmos, our spirits align. As the universe unfolds before us, in a tapestry of light and shade, In the heart of existence, our paths are laid.

Spheres of Existence

In the realm of the cosmos, where the fabric of existence is woven, We find our reflections in the stars, our destinies chosen. As we navigate the spectrum of being, where every light is a key, In the dance of the universe, our spirits are free.

VIBRATIONS

In the light of day, where the cosmos whispers tales of love, We find our harmony in the dance of the stars above. As the energy of the universe envelops us, in a cloak of light, In the heart of existence, our spirits take flight. In the essence of life, where the purity of water flows, We find our clarity in the crystal streams that glow. As the vibrations of the universe resonate, in every drop and wave, In the dance of existence, our spirits are brave. In the flow of the cosmos, where the energy of existence binds, We find our place in the universe, our spirits aligned. As the vibrations of creation resonate, in every atom and star, In the dance of the cosmos, we find who we are. In the essence of being, where the cosmos whispers tales of grace, We find our harmony in the simplicity of space. As the universe unfolds before us, in a tapestry of light and shade, In the heart of existence, our paths are laid. Beyond the bounds of time, where the cosmos stretches wide, We soar towards understanding, our spirits our guide. As the fabric of the universe weaves tales of light and dark, In the heart of existence, our journeys embark. In the realm of dreams, where the cosmos whispers secrets of old, We find our truths in the stories untold. As the universe unfolds before us, in a spectrum of light and shade, In the heart of existence, our paths are laid. In the twilight of existence, where the cosmos weaves tales of dusk, We find our moments of reflection, in the quiet hush. As the universe unfolds before us, in a spectrum of fading light, In the heart of existence, our spirits take flight In the dance of time, where the cosmos weaves tales of chance, we find our moments of reflection, in every chance. As the universe unfolds before us, in a spectrum of light and shade, In the heart of existence, our paths are laid.

Ascension

In the dance of the cosmos, where the fabric of existence is woven anew, We find our path towards enlightenment, our spirits true. As we align with the universe, our destinies unfold, In the heart of existence, our stories are told.

A Storm in the Sea

You came, then you departed, a fleeting presence in my heart, as a tempest rages across the sea, leaving traces of what used to be.

Winds of the Night

In the silent embrace of the night, the winds whisper secrets, Coming and going, a fleeting dance in the blink of an eye. They leave me standing on a path that beckons, the road calling, Heart leading, step by step, I traverse an endless sea of dreams.

In the tapestry of the night, promises glow like perfect light, Responsibility cradled in the hands destined to hold it right. Between you and me, real connections weave a tapestry of destiny, And I find solace in the ancient light that bathes us in its legacy.

Closer you draw, a vision that fills the gaps of longing, The distance narrows, illuminated by an ancient calling. In this dance of light and shadows, we find reconciliation, Becoming one, our spirits intertwine in harmonious celebration.

SWEET IS THE MELODY

I believe in the completeness of worlds within me, Where faith dances with dreams in an endless sea. Happiness, a whisper from your love, fills the void, My being resonates with the depth of the ocean, overjoyed. Sweet is the melody of your love that speaks to my core, Through the veil of the world, your essence I adore. Eternal memories etched in the fabric of our beings, I believe, as we meld, leaping beyond time, our spirits freeing. You and I, in a dance of liberation and return, Glimpsing eternity in each other's eyes, we learn. Losing everything only to find again, for a moment happiness seems reborn in the light, free from pain. Circles in time, our destinies interlaced, In the dance of letting go, in love we are encased. Breaking away, yet drawn back by a thread so fine, In this dance of freedom and fate, your heart meets mine. Believing in legends, possibilities akin? Survival, a testament to the ages we've seen, Tidal waves of love flood the space between. Remembering the word, the promise of you and me, through victories and losses, in love, we are free. As the world turns, our hearts hold fast, In dreams, in hope, in love that will last. All I am, all you are, in the vastness of being, In the dance of the cosmos, it's only you I'm seeing. As we align, guidance from above, clear and bright, Tomorrow's promise on the horizon, beyond the night.

www.ingramcontent.com/pod-product-compliance
Lightning Source LLC
Chambersburg PA
CBHW051232120626
46547CB00013B/1616